William Thughts

By AW Jackson

I hope this book inspires you!

Yours truly,
AW Jackson

Copyright © 2020 AW Jackson

All rights reserved.

This book is a work of fiction. All characters, names, locations, and references are a part of the author's imagination. Any similarities are purely coincidental.

Contact: AW Jackson
Email: **williamthughts@gmail.com**
Instagram: William_thughts
Facebook Page: William Thughts

Website: www.williamthughts.com

RCS Publishing, Leah G. Reynolds
Rcspublishingandmediagrp.com

Dedication

This book is dedicated to the loving memory of my grandmother, Peggy Lee Curtis.

Thank you for being my inspiration.

Acknowledgments

I would like to thank my mother, The Educator, The Young Godfather, SP Da Ghost, DJ, Howard Malik, and Mrs. Robinson you all have inspired and motivated me for greatness.

Dedication	3
Acknowledgments	4
Introduction	8
Basquiat	9
Soul Utopia	10
Hallucinations	11
Solibatio '03	12
Life	13
Dali	15
William's Intermission	16
Affair Confessions	17
A Woman I Admire	18
Unpredictable	19
Origami Woman	20
Left on Read	21
In My Feelings	22
William's Despair	23
Note to Self	24
St. Andrew	25
Action Is Bond	26
Black Terror	27
Fall Walker	28
Misjudgment	29
Self-Critic	30

Thughts 31

First Impression 32

I Use To Know You 33

Harry W. Nice Memorial Bridge 34

William's Head Space 35

Blue Raspberry Lemonade 36

Tran of Thught 37

Lee 39

Consistency 40

Tug of War 41

William's Onyx Humanity 42

HeEmotions 43

Aristotle 44

Abbey Slave Master 45

Unchained But Still a Slave 46

Complexion 47

Million Man March 48

Alcatraz 49

Assumption Bias 50

Glassdoor 51

William's Antidote 52

Social Media 53

Eddy William 54

5:20 AM 55

Graphyporn	57
Road Map to Nowhere	58
Unfinished Business	59
Elevated Embodiment	60
One Two Three	61
Stray Jacket	62
Stoned on U St	63
William's Afterpiece	64
Truth Hurts	65
Optimism	66
Tennis Court	67
Aspire	68
Nature's Bliss	69
Color Emotions of Life	70
DMV	71
Baffled Observation	72
Delusional Wonderland	74
Abstract Dreaming	76
True Definition of Happiness	77
Who Is William?	78
Sneak Peek	79
Male Survey	80

Introduction

William Thughts is a collection of poems that I have compiled to share with you. I invite you to escape inside my world to read, recite, and digest each line of text. Poetry gives us the most intimate way to relate with each other.

My work delves deep into life, love, and the empowerment of my people.

The first set of poems are a reflection of my mental state at the time. Basquiat is my introductory poem because it stands out to me as my moment of transformation. In this poem, I wrestled with self-esteem issues regarding the opposite sex. Contrary to the myth, most men are shy when it comes to approaching a woman. I attribute a lot of the initial intimidation to the lack of a strong male figure to model.

When I first wrote, Soul Utopia, I was struggling with negative self-talk and depression. Poetry was my only outlet, and so I began to write. Several poems were birthed from this period in my life. Witness the evolution.

Basquiat

Woman with the ugly hat
    I approach but don't
Maybe on a happier day, I would
    I'm discouraged, but I'm confident
I'm a nerd, but I'm popular
    I smile but don't
Maybe on a gloomy day, I would
    It's a nice day but its pouring raining
So I don't talk, but I speak
    She smiles but doesn't
Maybe on a sunny day, she would

Soul Utopia

Blinded by trees overshadowed by the Sea
Chilled sharp wind hard to believe it's a Breeze
Foggy mountaintops peaking in the distance barely to See
Shallow wavy water which reflection of Me
Shallow meaning my life and what it could Be
Vivid clear skies clear enough to see Lee
Rusty chipped door lock missing a Key
Rusty meaning my gifts that I can no longer use given by He
Bold, obnoxious plants the greenest tone of Tea
Strong rocky cliffs resemble We
But alone I stand soft equivalent to Brie

Hallucinations

Dark shadows at night filled my room
A little light shone through my window
I used to be afraid of the dark
But now it doesn't bother me

A little light shone through my window
I can barely see my hand in front of my face
But now it doesn't bother me
That my door is closed

I can barely see my hand in front of my face
I can barely see the outline
That my door is closed
Making the room more dark

I used to be afraid of the dark
When I was little
All I remember when I was younger was
Dark shadows at night filled my room

Solibatio '03

Things seemed so simple way back then
    No pressures. No insecurities
    Cyberbullying was non-existent
    Cell phones were unthought of
    Life was lax and drama free
    I was active back then
    Not sexually but athletically

Little League. Community Service. Stethem. Wade.

That's all I knew
An era where trying your best was good enough
And DID matter
Friendships and relationships were cherished
I remember way back then

Life

As a child growing up everything was so simple, filled with positive energy
Parents telling their kids, "you can be whatever you want to be in life Johnny all you have to do is try your best and work hard."

Johnny having a smile as wide as the Blue Ridge Mountains
Believing all is possible if he just works hard
As little Johnny gets older, the world shows signs of negative energy
The older Johnny got the more reality sets in his mind and thought process

Everyday life experiences makes Johnny not have that little Johnny mentality he once knew and was familiar with
School gets tougher; money gets tighter, love gets complicated life gets harder

Reality sets into Johnny soul while going through these life experiences and being very observant
Seeing others struggle who are the hardest workers in the world

While others who are lazy and still get everything their heart desires

From that day forth Johnny doesn't believe if you do everything in your power and will that you will be successful

Because sometimes you still might fall short
Johnny's deepest fear is that he might fall short of his goals and dreams no matter how hard he tries
Just take Johnny back to when he was a child growing up when life was so plain and simple

Dali

This fear has suddenly struck me since I gotten older
I don't want to face reality I want to be in a fantasy
A time period in the past instead of the present
A world where nothing gets old and people and things stay the same
Nothing dies and Nothing rots
Hair doesn't turn gray, and ages doesn't rise
No type of aches and pains and physical change
Everything just remains the same
I know I will go through this at one point in my life and
It's coming faster than I can handle
The ball is coming too fast for me to hit it out of the park
I can't handle how fast this is moving
I think about it, and I want to cry because I know deep down
inside its right around the corner
I know it's something I can't control
No one can
I can't change the future yet to come

William's Intermission

Since I can remember, I have been fascinated by the female form, their attitude, their scent, and the way their hips sway when they walk. My relationships and interactions with the women in my life have become a muse for writing. There is no one who loves you more than your woman. She makes sure that you are fed, taken care of, and nurtured with love.

I've dedicated the next section of poems to the women who have had an impact on my life. Whether they have cared for me, loved me, or ultimately broken me, I still love women without abandon.

The more I grow and learn, the more I recognize where I could have done better by the women I dated and were involved in relationships. I feel like I have come to a point where I can take ownership for my part in the destruction of certain relationships.

In the poem, "Affair Confessions," I write my personal apology to the hearts that I have wounded while I was in the process of finding myself.

Affair Confessions

I'm sorry Puzzle Piece maybe I could have been there more

I'm sorry Graphic Design maybe I should have been less forgiving

I'm sorry Chestnut Hill maybe I should have been more private

I apologize Emotions maybe I should have gave it a chance

I apologize Aquarius maybe I should have been more positive

I'm sorry Cacao maybe I should have been more understanding

I'm sorry Educator maybe I should have been less draining and patient

Maybe it's me
We'll see

A Woman I Admire

To a woman I adore
I see the beauty in your inner soul and so much more
Before you came into my life, life was a bore
But since you came into my life, I get a warm more than satisfying feeling deep in my core
The way you make me feel as if I just scored, the winning basket but instead of getting a trophy I won your heart
I don't know what drives me so crazy about you
Is it your beauty? How your teeth and smile are perfect, so innocent but so bold
Or is it your personality that shines brighter than any sunlight reflecting off the shore
Maybe it's your wild natural full hair imitating how crazy you can get
Maybe it's because how I am so amazed on how you carry yourself
It might be because I see the passion and worry you have for me deep in your round brown caring eyes
You are my needle in the hay stack; you're very rare and hard to find
But I found you; we found each other
Because no one is as special and precious as you
Us being with each other look how much we grew closer to each other
You're my best friend
When I'm with you, I never want it to end
I trust and love you more than anyone before
So this is for the woman I adore

Unpredictable

Your eyes twinkle like the moon at night, while it shines off the lake
I see you staring deeply into my eyes
I want to know what you're thinking like a psychiatrist
Are we still going to be together five years from now?
Life is unpredictable like Heaven or Hell; you don't know where you're going to end up at
I grab your hand and its cold like ice

I look into his eyes so deeply I can see the reflection of my eyes in his
Your eyes are as small and well rounded like two dimes
I wonder what he is thinking
I am curious like a toddler
Are you thinking about us?
Are we still going to be attracted to each other three years from now?
Life is hard like a granite rock
I grab his hand, and it's hot like fire

Origami Woman

Dark, twisted soul I can't unfold
Twisted dark soul I can't ignore
Cause I crave for more
Stress frustration depression soul as he
Depression frustration stress as she
Illusion drugs self-hate
Self- hate and illusions from the drugs that he intakes
Confusion sadness he seeks love from this dark, twisted soul
But this dark, twisted soul makes love be filled with sadness and confusion
Annoying repetitive chain of events keep playing in my memory
Repetitive, annoying chain of events actually keeps on happening
With this dark, twisted soul I can't ignore but
I crave for more

Left on Read

Dig deep down in my pages to fully get the autobiography
Pull out my core like biting into a peach
Let the conversation flow consuming the space like pouring a glass of water
Accept my letter of morals and standards like college
My message was read, but she didn't respond

In My Feelings

Deserted on an island isolated from snow
Nowhere to plant my seeds in order to grow
No nutritions, no sunlight, no water to fill my pain
Mentally in my head, I'm going insane
No one will get it nor understand my struggles
These same struggles causes me to put up this bubble
Trying to protect myself from these predictable emotions
No wait…..let me stay focus

William's Despair

Everyone has experienced pain, depression, and sadness. No matter who you are, you have been affected by both joy and pain. When emotions overwhelm me and take over my thoughts, I am drawn to write.

Poetry provides me with a method and means for an escape. I need to write like Eagles need to fly. It is not only my passion, writing is my life's purpose. When the daily toils become too much and I find myself alone with my thoughts, this is when beauty is born.

The alchemist does their best work with raw materials. What are we besides creatures driven by our emotions?

The next set of poems that you read were written during the times in my life when my emotions took full control of my art.

Note to Self

I look to the left and see nothing but emptiness and space between a tree
I look to my right and see cracks running down the sidewalk continuing on the street
I keep looking for something to happen or someone to show up, but nothing is there
Countless nights and endless conversations with a species that doesn't understand my intentions nor my existence of being there
    Maybe one day something magical will happen, and I will believe in the tooth fairy again
    But as the days go on and years go by, I often ask why?
    Does a creature even exist all I can do is sigh
Sigh so deep that it hurts my inner chest
    I often think I should just leave with no trace
Maybe that's best

St. Andrew

Fishing, just fishing in a shallow pond near me
Fishing, just fishing just sitting here I guess I got to wait and see
Fishing, just fishing truth be told I don't know how to fish at all
Fishing, just fishing starring at the water my reflection looks so tall
Fishing, just fishing impatiently waiting to get that tug on my line
Fishing, just fishing, is this what people really do?
Fishing, just fishing, wait! I think I got something I reel it in
Fishing, just fishing I pull it out it's a tiny fish
Fishing, just fishing I'm not pleased I throw it back in
Fishing, just fishing I'm much more patient now because I know how it feels to catch something
Fishing, just fishing, wait! I got something feels bigger than before
Fishing, just fishing I'm not impressed I throw it back in looking for more
Fishing, just fishing for days, months, and years at a time
Fishing, just fishing while my life is passing me by
Fishing......I'm just fishing

Action Is Bond

I see a soul that is gentle and shy as I
And wrongly treated by others and often asks why?
The pain I saw in your eyes that morning left you to cry
It cut so deep it was like I died
I just keep thinking why give up someone so special, that was so hard to find
Her beauty is overshadowed by her kind
Her kindness and passion I see in her character and walks of life
I hope I'm good enough to make her my wife
One day in due time I don't mean to scare you
But I know deep down in my heart I want you more each day
I lust for your mind and spirit
I desire your happiness and smile
I appreciate your morals and style
I see a woman that is selfless and strong as I

Black Terror

Having doubts trying to figure it out
Sleepless nights thinking out loud
Painful mornings trying to hide a frown
But deep down inside I'm broken
I don't know where to go or things to say to who
As I walk in the door dressed up if only they knew
Blinded by society, they have no clue
Oh, what should I do?

Reminiscing on decisions I made and my future mistakes
Confused about life and people and questioning what it takes
Or will I ever be happy? Will she ever be happy? Or is she even happy?
I would hope so because I'm doing the best I can
My mental pain overshadows my physical pain
It's a constant storm that always rains
And left there feeling sorrow with nothing to gain
Maybe it's just me, I shouldn't complain

Fall Walker

Tears filled my eyes making it
hard to swallow
Heartbroken and don't want to
see tomorrow
Aching heart I need someone's to
borrow
Oh what sweet sorrow
But at the same time I'm hurting
and don't want to bother
Oh my life feels fallow
Maybe I will try again tomorrow
Oh what sweet sorrow

Misjudgment

I once knew you long ago it was so clear to me

The people we believe in not as who they seem

Nothing but faith and joyful feelings only foreshadowing their soul

But just then only milliseconds go by, and they start to be cold

Life's too short for our souls to meet

And instantly our souls crumble in defeat

So discrete

Self-Critic

Is enough…enough?
Or is enough too much?
Even if enough is too little
But is it still enough?
Is enough a full effort?
Is your enough not enough effort?
Or does my enough outweighs your enough?
Does my enough make you happy?
Does your enough make me sad?
Is my enough bad?
Does my enough make you feel mad?
My enough is enough; I hope you feel the same
But if my enough isn't enough, am I the one to blame?

Thughts

I miss the old William
The always happy William
The always active William
The less distracted William

I know the caring William
The always smiling William
The always passionate William
The positive attitude William
The bend over backwards William

I miss the stuttering William
The always innocent William
Loved sleepovers William
Everybody knows William

I miss the sober William
The less moody William
The less stressed William
The less anxiety William

I miss the braces William
The always laughing William
The beautiful personality William
The always at tutoring William

But I don't know William
Will I ever meet William?
Will I ever know William?
Is William even William?

First Impression

I am who I tend to be, and that's between me and you
I am who I appear to be, is this really true?
I am who I want to be it's not fairly new
I am who I don't want to be doing things I don't normally do
I am who I envision to be causing my mind to be skew
I am who I need to be wanting people to see my hue
I am who I'm destined to be if only they knew
I am who I am someone like me is only few

I Use To Know You

Love
Hate
Dislike
Annoying
Rude, Selfish, Foolish
That's how I feel about her

Harry W. Nice Memorial Bridge

Intellectual beauty queen feeding my soul exactly what I need
Inspired by her greatness and drive not by her career but her drive for I
I can see this in your eyes the passion and your desire
When our souls meet its hot as the oven

But now you're cold as cement in the winter
You're as shallow as a kiddie pool
You're as rude as a school bully
You're as distant as the two different states we live in

William's Head Space

I have been surrounded by strong women throughout my life. I have the utmost respect for women and what they endure to provide for their families. I was raised by a single mother who gave her everything for me. I am both proud and impressed by my mother and my grandmother's strength and tenacity.

This collection of poems are inspired by my mother and my grandmother. In the poem "Blue Raspberry Lemonade," my mother was supporting both of us, and I knew that it wasn't an easy feat. My beloved grandmother passed away suddenly, and it truly broke my heart. I reflect on those moments of loss in the poem, "Lee." I am still healing from this tremendous loss.

I recall watching her one day as she paid out our bills, and I just knew that she was struggling. I was feeling down, as well. I remember walking inside the kitchen and opening the door to the refrigerator. Inside was a freshly made container of Blue Raspberry Lemonade Kool-Aid, and for the first time in a long time, I smiled to myself. It warmed my heart to know that even though my mother was going through it, she still took the time to make my favorite drink. Although the situation seemed small, that moment was one of the most significant of my life.

Blue Raspberry Lemonade

I'm in a mood that's undesirable when stepping foot in the house
In that next moment, my angel is off, something is odd
Feeling depressed, defeated, defenseless
Crying and frustrated, what went wrong?
Nowhere to run, no shelter to stay safe, no one to turn to for help
I'm the backbone now for my backbone is now broken and needs to be fix
I need this moment an opportunity to be first for once
I'm tired of losing the same race each and every year
I try to have hope, but I feel this time it's much different
This time there is no plan, there is no other option
I'm doing the best I can to look over my angel wishing I had the power and strength white people have
I leave my angel to get ready, and I look in the fridge
I see the blue Kool-Aid sitting there
And I smile

Tran of Thught

Sitting here thinking to my lonesome
I've been calling you because I feel like I'm chosen
I'm the one supposed to prosper
But really am I? You making life so much harder
I know I didn't deserve this pain neither did my provider
I just think it's fucked up how I'm calling you, but you don't talk back
But you talking to others that's living the life full of sin
I don't understand
I thought if I do everything the right way things would be more positive instead of negative
Ever since you took one of the greatest creations you ever made from me, I don't know
I just don't know…
Everything is even more blurry and disoriented
I can't see shit!
She is stumbling and weakening even more now than ever before each and everyday
Truth be told I'm scared

Scared of losing her or her losing herself
Things changed in a blink of an eye...so quick
I don't recognize her no more, that's scary to say
I don't recognize myself no more, that's shameful to say
It's like she is hanging from a rope by her remains
How can we sustain a positive mind frame?

Lee

Over the hills overshadow by trees I see Lee
My Precious Gracious Lee
Oh thee how my Lee was good to me
As I lay my head to sleep, I smell Lee
Your smell was so comforting and soothing
Oh what an innocent smell it was Lee
As I sit in quiet and stillness in the chair, I remember as if it was yesterday of Lee
Oh, how He took away my Lee!
My Precious Gracious Lee
Oh thee how my Lee was good to me

Consistency

The world is dark and dim filled with sin
Still faces in the shadows all I see are grins
Smirks getting wider, louder, increasing in volume
In pure darkness feels as if I'm being followed
Followed by stereotypes, double standards, judgment, traditions
My vision of the world is much more vivid
Much more detail to even explain
Sometimes I even get lost in what I'm trying to say
I do know one thing I will always remain the same
No amount of money will cause me to change
Or switch lanes on the people leaving them astray

Tug of War

¿Why should I find the time
But¿   during that time I find
    Inspirations ¿ and negativity
¿But having   negativity   in my inspirations
Cause   ¿stress and anxiety
¿Too much   anxiety causes stress
To my health and my view¿   on life
Having life   ¿changes my view on health
Having health changes   ¿my view on wealth
But   ¿ having wealth changes my view on life

William's Onyx Humanity

Being a black man living in this great country, I have faced racism, stereotyping, and prejudices throughout my life. From my time in Catholic school all the way to the working world, I am constantly reminded that the color of my skin matters.

The incessant reminders and racial injustices have irritated me to the point of becoming raw. My rawness is what you will find in the next selection of poems. Black men are often portrayed as hard, emotionally stunted, and angry because our emotional vulnerabilities are rarely exposed. You will not find us crying about the trauma we have faced. We are taught to hold it all in and pretend as if nothing affects our spirits and soul.

There is such great importance placed on racial biases that were constructed long before you and I existed. This next section is dedicated to Black Empowerment, the appreciation of Black emotion and the acceptance of Black thought.

HeEmotions

If I was **White**, I would have all the opportunities
If I was **Spanish**, I would have a strong relationship with my family
If I was **Jewish**, I would have a lot of money
If I were a **pro athlete**, I would have all the women
If I were a **woman**, I would have all the sympathy from society
If I were **African**, I would have a stable job
If I were **Indian**, I would have my own business
If I had a **career**, I would be respected
If I was **rich**, I would have a voice
If I had a **child**, I would have a purpose
If I had a **hobby**, I would have a passion
If I had **power**, I would be important
But I have none of these things
I'm just a Black man

Aristotle

The higher I climb, the more I feel left behind
The more I see, the more knowledge I can achieve
The more I fall, the tougher I become
The more I listen, the wiser I became
The more I was observant, the more I understood
The more I heard others, the more I understand

Abbey Slave Master

Why I feel such a discomfort when walking into this room
Not just any room this specific room
This specific class
I didn't know having class was bad
Why do I have to be the voice for my people?
I speak, and my family is quiet
I'm calling for backup, but I have none
I'm not here to impress nobody
Save face or how I'm perceived

Fast forward later in time
Why I feel such disappointment when walking the crowded street
Not just this specific street but all streets
I didn't know having morals was bad
Why do I have to be the voice for His people?
I speak, and society is mute
I don't need backup anymore
I'm not here to follow suit
Follow traditions or chattel
Fast forward to now

Unchained But Still a Slave

Servant I see but servant I be
  Washing the windows to be free
    Free indeed it be if it was just me
      But me feeling free would be indeed
        Starring out these windows the same windows I cleaned
          Wishing I could read
           Seeing I could see
            Being I could be

Complexion

Blurred color visions steady trying to focus
Lost in one's thoughts confused on my emotions
Steady pushing down the twisted road and it's golden
I am the one chosen

Million Man March

I am your ear to listen to all your problems and struggles
I am your voice to speak up and defend yourself when you're afraid to
I am your eyes to look away when negativity that comes your way
I am your feet to walk away from violence and conflict situations
I am your shoulder to cry on when you feel lonely and don't have support
I am your smile you show the world even though you are going through hardships
I am your hands to pick you up when you are down
I am your knees to stand up for what is right despite how others feel or think
I am your brain to keep being strong mentally and keep pushing yourself to fulfill your goals
I am a Black man

Alcatraz

I'm a slave to living
I'm a slave to life
I'm a slave to happiness
I'm a slave to relationships
Why does society influence the greater outcome of how I should feel about them?
Or determines what it should look, feel, or sound like

You're a slave to family
You're a slave to perception
You're a slave to double standards
You're a slave to careers
Why does society influence the greater outcome of how you should feel about me?

Assumption Bias

It was a still and gloomy day but I was still protected by the sun rays
This sufficient chain of events it's hard to even say
This runs deeper than me even deeper than ecosystems and trees
This runs further deeper than a cold winter night causing everything to freeze
This pain runs deeper than me getting on my knees
Apologizing for things I didn't mean
This is not what it seems
But let me get back to the seize
Of events that troubled me
A pain so deep and involuntarily it feels I'm being smothered
A pain that cuts even more deeper it's as if you were my brother
This confusion and hurt is like no other
Because my real intentions is I'm just here to support my mother
Then the man with power that looked just like me asks, "what is your case number?"

Glassdoor

I see on the other side how happiness should be
I see on the other side what happiness is
I see on the other side of how she truly feels about me
I see on the other side my self worth
I see on the other side my self hurt
I see on the other side my self pain
I see on the other side my self-shame
I seen on the other side how selfish people are
I seen on the other side how society corrupted us all
I seen on the other side the lies she told me
I seen on the other side how death can destroy a family

William's Antidote

Have you ever wanted something so badly that you were willing to do anything to get it? Was there someone in your life whom you were unwilling to give up even though they were bad for you?

This is how addiction feels. Addiction has been associated with drugs for so long that many don't understand how they could be addicted to an object, an affection or a person. Have you ever been addicted?

Of course, you have. Addiction to sugar, soda, food, money, love, Facebook and Instagram likes, followers, fame, etc. The list could go on for an eternity. We also become addicted to emotions. Our pain, trauma, and suffering are addictive emotions. We become so used to the pain that we talk about it, rehearse it, and think about it like a drug.

The following poems are about addictions and the emotional drain that comes along with loving something or someone that slowly destroys you.

Social Media

Emotional stress as to one's intentions or motives
Constant feelings on cloud nine then drastically lows, lower than the soil
Pressures how one should look like or envy others passions
When something happens acts are drastic
Mentally this is fact this is law
Seesaw of emotions feeling hot then cold
Confused on what to do, questioning their existence
Questioning my existence
Questioning

Eddy William

That's all I think about
That sensation that is like no other
Drowning out the world, well at least trying to
I think I'm addicted to that feeling
The feeling where I'm coming out of my body nothing but a soul is left
I feel the music and beat go through my core; I love that feeling
1800 is my favorite number
Mixed with citrus juices
In the dark night swerving on the highway dodging speed cameras
I'm not myself I'm someone else
Without care, without fear, without insecurities, without problems
Wait I'm lying about insecurities
I know I need to stop
But it's hard

5:20 AM

I feel so bad that I don't think about you as much as I should
I feel even worse not visiting you barely at all
I really want to, but life is hitting me hard....hitting us hard
Do you remember me? Because I know I remember you
Do you still love me?
Because I know I still love you
I could still smell your scent for the first month in your room
Oh how I loved your scent
Laying on your bed, relaxing, talking to you about my relationship problems
You understood me, motivated me, inspired me, gave me strength, healed me
Oh how you made me so mad
Furious...I wish I could be mad at you
I often walk past and see you sitting there staring at me
It use to creep me out and made me sad
I miss helping you
Like cleaning up and organizing your closet, help putting on your socks
I was so selfish I couldn't see how bad it was getting

I was blinded because you were my best friend, my hero
You still are
It's true what they say "no matter how it plans out, life goes on."
I never understood that till it happened to me...
No wait I never felt that until it happened to me
But I'm glad it happened, you needed a break emotionally, physically, and mentally
I will see you soon coach

Graphyporn

Desires that run deeper than the human eye can see
Elementary I was first introduced
It started in high school....no wait in college
The more I saw, the more I wanted it from a special person
Satisfying in the beginning stages but now it's just something to do
Chasing a high you can never reach
It's nothing like the first time, the first actual experience
But now it's not satisfying; it's not fulfilling especially during the dry seasons
An addiction that runs deeper than the human eye can see
An addiction that lies in me

Road Map to Nowhere

Darkness in all places where no light is shone
Blindness in all aspects and can't see where to go
Going through your whole life with the answers to your questions are no
Not giving you the opportunity to grow
But when I look at myself, I'm much smarter than you think you know
Scared to express myself to show
My self worth is……..

Unfinished Business

We use to kick it like DC United
This sudden urge I cannot fight it
I was lost, but now I'm enlightened
No other human gets me excited

Now we don't speak like the relationship with my father.

Elevated Embodiment

Abyss of mist surround by seas
Of a numbness of pain that feels me
A pain so deep and distinct it's hard to even swallow
But this same pain makes people feel not as shallow
My body feels like cement all I can do is stare
I feel content when the stress of this world is unable to bare
A grinding sensation twists my chest with annoyance and persistent repetition
Daily routines the vaguest of them all seems like a mission
But this same pain makes me have a connection with you
But even when I'm with you, I still feel alone making me feel it's one instead of two

One Two Three

I see We but can it Be?
I see You, but it's just I
I see This, but it's That
I want Us, but it's just Me
I want two, but it's three

Stray Jacket

These drugs help me stay sane
Helps me coup with the wild things surfacing in my membrane
The harsh pain I wish it was vague
But it's too powerful to maintain
Day to day life's a strain
Anxiety and frustration of what my life has remained
My mind is hard to maintain
I think I'm going insane

Stoned on U St

Numbness and a heavy tingling sensations feel my core
The lower I get I desire for more
Wishing that all this pain will just wash away from shore
Feeling no purpose of life and it's a bore
No matter how much strength I use I can't turn the door
To the happiness of my life no matter how hard I try
Cautiously looking around watching everyone pass me by
But once I take this special potion, I can now fly
I continue to eat feeling alive, but also it makes me feel I'm about to die
All at the same time
My mental state says it's only right, but I know it's a lie

William's Afterpiece

Life takes different twists and turns as we navigate towards our own version of happiness. On my quest for joy I have found that a small amount of sadness comes along with elated joy. We must first experience the bad to appreciate the good in life. I feel like I have done just that with my existence.

Just like one of my favorite poet's Edgar Allen Poe, there is a solitary theme throughout this book and an undercurrent of emotion that I hope you all feel.

Although we all have faced different challenges and experiences in life how we apply the lessons from the pain is the key. I have turned my pain into optimism and dedication. I know that the greatness that is meant for me is heading my way. I have no reason to stress.

I want to share with you some of these emotions, these feelings of joy and pain. It is my hope that you catch a glimpse inside of my heart to see William's joy.

Truth Hurts

Am I the person that I'm meant to be?
To she, I am greatness, nice, caring
Go out of my way for anyone and anything at any given time
Maybe that's a lie
I look in the mirror and see nothing feel nothing
Life and circumstances causes me to feel this way
Sadness and sorrow causes you to hurt and feel pain towards others you can't explain
OR refrain from telling the truth cause you already know what will remain
You by yourself all by your lonesome
Sometimes it's them, but mostly it's me

Optimism

Even though we fight and fuss I still believe in us
I still believe in you and I even if it's a lack of trust
We have to let go of our pride and show the same bond as the days we first laid eyes
On one another and our strong connection didn't die
That us not seeing eye to eye doesn't take away from our highs
That we know and understand by having one another that's the true prize
Even though it might be in disguise
I want our love for one another to stretch as far as the skies
I want our love to be as soft and sweet as your beautiful thighs
I want our love to nigh

Tennis Court

Stuck in a place called no man's land
It's hard to move and unsure where to go
No person to turn to, to call one's home
Not literally a home but a person I feel safe with and protect me
Physically no…Mentally yes
I feel lost and alone more than ever
Its good qualities and bad qualities about the situation
 It feels like I'm stuck like plaster. I mean, I could leave, but what else would I have?
Who would I talk to now?
Who would I express my love intimately with?
Who would be my best friend and care about me more than just a "friend"?
It's tiresome starting over in life
It's exhausting making others see what you see and feel what you feel
Or proving something is real
That's just how I feel

Aspire

It's cold on the floor
But hot in the air
The wind rips the souls causing them to tear
Into bits and pieces of unforgotten mysterious
The mystery of the connection between you and me
Between you and I, I starred as I laid eyes
On the last time, we met both of our emotions cried
The happiness and joyful of such a presence causes all pain to vanish
The willingness and her passion causes me to soar even when
I'm cold as the floor once stated before
Her love is something I can't ignore
I strive forth

Nature's Bliss

Soft shapeless, small grains
  Of sand blowing on the beach
Falling threw my hand

Color Emotions of Life

Green.
Money, Life, Plants, Grass, Growth

Blue.
Scared, Sorrow, Loneliness, Defeat, Sadness

Yellow.
Joy, Excitement, Passion, Anxious, Happiness

Red.
Angry, Heated, Hatred, Jealousy, Pain

Black.
Emptiness, Stillness, Discolored, Lifeless, Death

Pure, Clean, Doves, Heaven, Rebirth

DMV

Two states and a city
Similarities in culture and background
Equal tran of thought and mindset
Suburbs and city life within reach
Many jobs but barely any opportunities
Distinct accents and slang terminology

New Balances, Foams, Jordans, Helly Hanson, GSTAR,
Diesel, Backyard, Kevin Durant
Crime rate high, murder rate higher

Walking to get around and Metro to commute
I live in the middle of a city and a state
DC, Maryland, Virginia

Baffled Observation

Why not show how much you care for someone instead of hiding your emotions from them
Why not want the best for people instead of wanting the worse for them
Why not give someone your last if they never had a first
Why not be happy for others even if you're not happy at the moment
Why not smile finding out that someone is happy or excited
Why not be proud and satisfied about other people's relationships and marriages instead of hating on what they have
Why not stop someone from doing wrong
Why not stop violence being done instead of just letting it happen
Why not be bold and speak up when someone or something is wrong instead of just sitting back and saying nothing
Why not congratulate someone on their accomplishments instead of being jealous of what they have fulfilled
Why not help someone without expecting anything in return
Why not be honest with someone in the beginning, so you don't waste their time at the end
Why not inspire others to be better than and just as successful as you, if not more

Why not be a role model to others not just to the people that are younger than you
Why not show someone how to do something instead of expecting them to know how to do it
Why not be yourself instead of following others interests, beliefs, and morals
Why not live your own life and not others life
Why not boost someone's idea or thought up instead of shutting it down
Why not protect people from getting hurt but instead you hurt people because it happened to you
Why not compliment someone on their clothes, shoes, appearance or inner soul rather than just stealing, being envious, and jealous of others
Why not be happy because you're alive and living rather than being mad at what you don't have
Why not speak to everyone that comes your way instead of having your head down going right past them
Why not?

Delusional Wonderland

What is the true meaning of it?
A bright surreal fantasy that only exist in one person's dreams
Where everything and everyone are so perfect, nice, and friendly
Everyone looking and sounding the same with the same physical and emotional features
No negative but only positives vibes
A state of being where we think it's a lie and could never be reachable
Seeing others and believe that's what it truly is or that's what it feels like
Causing your mind to be blind and foggy and only see how others think it may be or how should it feel
A nice lavish lifestyle where you can get whatever your heart desires

Money, shoes, clothes, cars, jewelry, infinity amount of men or women swarming at your feet
Having the perfect body to be considered beautiful or appealing to others
Having priceless intangible things that we deeply care about such as
Family, kids, friends, love ones, pets
People or things we form a strong bond with causing us to smile uncontrollably
A satisfied soul where it's calm, peaceful, and simple
Where what matters most is striving for success no matter what the outcome maybe
Always giving it your all developing content ness with life and what it has to offer
Having a special creature completing you caring deeply for you even more than their own self
Having the exact same morals and mindset, you both possess
When you look in the mirror, you see that person as your reflection
What we are desperate to find but it's difficult to obtain
Happiness.

Abstract Dreaming

Blue lagoon swirling in this monsoon
Deep-sea diving in the abyss of a pool
Swirling Twirling Twisters fill my room
Musical singing-dancing brooms
Wild, crazy tree branches forming a house
Fury quiet creature that lived in this house was a mouse
Misty fluffy clouds surrounding my space forming a bed
in which I lay
Freshest and ripest fruit I ever seen even more vivid
Surrounding and overseeing this fruit is a 12-foot snake
making me timid
To taste this glorious magical sensation of a fruit
In the foggy distance, it's a bare naked chocolate woman
playing a flute
Magical smoothest most beautiful tune I to ever hear
At the same time, a storm was approaching from the rear
Of my bedroom and I sit still sitting in the dark
Thinking.

True Definition of Happiness

Peacefully she is watching over me

Every day I think about you, happily that your soul is finally set free

Grandparent I loved and cherished with glee

Gentle and wise is she

Young to me physically but mentally strong as a tree

Loving me unconditionally on this earth

Ensuring my well-being and taking care of me since birth

Enormous heart, she had and showed us how much we are worth

Conversations we had were timeless

Understanding of one another made our moments priceless

Relationship with you was special and righteous

Transparent about all problems of life even when I thought it was lightless

Independent woman and your personality filled the room with brightness

Shining a light through the clouds of heaven and God is your pilot

Who Is William?

Driven by raw emotion and a passion for writing, AW has penned his feelings for over a decade. Encouraged by his grandmother's tenacity and wisdom, he was determined to succeed. Combining the love for sports and the gift of writing, AW's first short story soared to the top of the list. He received recognition, and his debut book was published while he was still in Elementary school.

As he matured, AW grew more aware of the injustices that occurred to those who had no voice. Poised to give a voice to the heartache, pain, and suffering of those around him, AW has penned over sixty poems.

AW's writing style has evolved from the love of sports to the allure and intrigue of love itself. He delves into the societal troubles that currently plague our community, such as drugs, hate, prejudice, and pain.

Using the alchemy of poetry, AW turned pain into purpose to create poems that will keep you thinking, feeling, and inspired.

Sneak Peek

Check out the latest poem from my future release which is due to be out in April 2021.

www.williamthughts.com

Male Survey

A women that's drama free that lifts me in high spirits in my time of need
A gentle and soft spoken creature guiding me at times when I'm unable to see
One that is distance and fades away past the mountain tops but enough to see the outline of her soul through the mist and fog
Willing to be grownup to to admit when she is wrong
Who doesn't mind trading in her dollar for my quarter when I don't have it
But is still willing to turn down my quarter when I'm down to my last cent

Made in the USA
Columbia, SC
08 June 2020